Transformation
discover
your own flight pattern

Shannon M. Tobin

Library of Congress Cataloging-in-Publication Data

Shannon M Tobin,
Transformation: Discover Your Own Flight Pattern
Edited by: Karen R. Thomas, and Jill Ellis
Published by: Soul Writers, LLC: PO Box 291835 Tampa, FL 33687

ISBN: 978-0-9844822-7-6

10 9 8 7 6 5 4 3 2 1

Printed in the United States of America

Note: This book is intended only as an informative guide for those wishing to know about love. Readers are advised to consult a professional relationship coach or counselor before making any changes in their love life. The reader assumes all responsibility for the consequences of any actions taken based on the information presented in this book. The information in this book is based on the author's research and experience. Every attempt has been made to ensure that the information is accurate; however, the author cannot accept liability for any errors that may exist. The facts and theories on love and relationships are subject to interpretation, and the conclusions and recommendations presented here may not agree with other interpretations.

Emerge Into Your
Greatness!

Freedom.... to be, to do, to have, to live, to give and to receive.

One of the greatest challenges in life is being yourself in a world that's trying to make you like everyone else. You don't have to settle; it's simply a choice you make every day.

It's time to reclaim your life, discover and live in your purpose - for what you do, for who you are, for what you stand for.

My vision and purpose is to inspire, motivate and move you to accept and embrace the beauty of your defects and know that your greatest strengths lie in who you already are!

Never change who you are,
but change what you do, so you can
'Be' who you are!

~Shannon M. Tobin

A SOULWRITERS PUBLICATION

I DEDICATE THIS BOOK TO MY SON, COLE

You are the fuel in my engine that keeps it running. You make me want to be a better person.

I admire your giving heart and your brave sense of spirit, which propels you to live out loud and be your authentic self. You remind me, daily, of the importance of this, and I thank you for that.

It's so evident that you have the vision to change the world with your servant mentality.

I'm so proud of the young man you're becoming. I now see that my number one role as your mom is to empower you with a vision to change the world by showing you how to seize God's vision for your life.

Table of Contents

Introduction

By Jenni Mudge-Winters

I'll never forget the day that the trajectory of my life changed. "You don't remember me, do you?" the woman in front of me said excitedly. Her energy and enthusiasm was so contagious that it made me laugh.

That was the day God put Shannon Tobin and I back in each others' lives. Now we know why and what this meeting has done for both of us.

The last few years have been a roller coaster of a ride - with digging deep, being raw, facing the mirror - all the while watching the heart of an amazingly authentic woman emerge, understanding full well that peaks come with valleys. The beauty of this ride has been that every step of the way Shannon sought the lessons, always sharing her learning freely with others. This book is a testament to that.

Freedom is not letting your yesterday affect your today.

Shannon, thank you for giving the world this precious gift and sharing your transformation in words. You truly are standing in your power and purpose. Mary Kay Ash (founder of Mary Kay Cosmetics) is looking down with a wide smile and her heart singing knowing that you are leading by example and enriching the lives of women, as you have mine. I plan to pass these blessings on to others!

I'm truly blessed and grateful to be on this journey with you, my coach, my spiritual mentor and most of all my sister-friend!

Jenni Mudge-Winters is an Independent Sales Director Mary Kay Cosmetics

Prologue

By Madhumita Lama

A successful, strong and confident businesswoman was my first impression of Shannon Tobin when we met at a Mary Kay meeting. She was an amazing speaker, full of energy and enthusiasm. But beyond this I had also felt an instantaneous connection with her.

As I spent more time with her, I felt that I could be myself. I was going through a tough personal crisis. Having lived my life filled with self-pity, I was strict with myself, depriving myself of anything that felt good. I feel that my outlook stemmed from the less than perfect life I grew up in. A 'small voice' kept nudging me to bare my soul to Shannon, and when I listened to that little voice it was like suddenly all of my worries and concerns magically faded into oblivion. She helped me realize that the answer was right there in front of me and helped me bring back my confidence. Today I am a strong and confident person, ready to start my journey to make a positive difference in my own life, in the lives of those around me and in the larger world.

Shannon seems to possess many qualities of Jetsun Dolma, one of the female goddesses in Buddhism. Being a Buddhist, this likeness struck me mightily. Dolma represents the virtues of success in work and achievements, enlightened activity, compassion, power of healing and serenity. She is also believed to attract all good things, including power, wealth and prosperity. Much is praised about her strength and beauty. I do not hesitate to say that I see the true manifest of Drolma in Shannon. Like they say, God lives amongst us, so after this I would not agree any less.

During the darkest hours of my life, Shannon's concern for me, her words of hope and love, her words of acceptance, courage and support, and, at times, her mere presence helped me from slipping away forever.

May you carry on achieving the pinnacles of success in all your endeavours, Shannon, and with this book, may you go on blessing the lives of many in need like you have blessed mine!

Note To the Reader

When I see a butterfly flying, it reminds me of the miracle of my life: change and flight.

The metaphor of the butterfly's transformation is profound:

The caterpillar that is kind of banal looking becomes the beautiful, radiant butterfly.

Before the caterpillar becomes a butterfly, it prepares its cocoon as though it were dying. What the caterpillar thinks is the end of its life is really the beginning.

The caterpillar knows intuitively and in alignment with nature when it is time to start spinning its bed to sleep in. You do not see other caterpillars walking over, tapping them on the shoulder saying, "It is time, you are ready." It is intuitive. Change is intuitive. So many people are waiting for permission to fight for their dreams. Someone to validate them, tell them they could do it. However, the path is clearest when the knowing is intuitive.

The caterpillar sheds its old skin, which forms the chrysalis cocoon and goes inward for a few days. (For some of us mammals, this could be weeks, months or years.)

The caterpillar does not go inside the cocoon and unzip its caterpillar suit for a butterfly suit. He becomes a big puddle of liquid that some affectionately refer to as a digestive soup. This liquid chooses parts of the caterpillar to hold onto and kills off the rest. Then, it creates new butter-fly tissue.

The butterfly then has to fight, and fight hard, to get himself out of the chrysalis. Moreover, if someone tries to help the butterfly out, it dies. It's the process of working to get out that gives it the strength and development time that it needs to actually survive.

Then the butterfly is ready to learn to walk, and then fly.

What a powerful metaphor!

Where are you in your life? Are you a butter-fly, soaring, enjoying your elegant manifestation? Are you a caterpillar getting the message that it is time to transition - time to do something differ-ent? Are you lying in a puddle of what once was you and what may be the future you? Are you sit-ting around and waiting for someone to give you permission or affirmation of your next step on your path? Are you looking at what would need to happen to get you out of your shell and coding it "hard work," which makes you disinclined to act on it? Alternatively, are you seeing the obsta-cles as learning experiences – pathways to your own inner strength and mastery?

Is it time to step fully and completely into the new version of you? That means letting go of ev-erything in your life that is not serving you. You do not have to do it all at once. Just take the first step. Do the first thing. The rest will follow, and with each step forward you will feel more em-powered. You will find that you are supported.

It can be scary and painful at first, but know you're not alone.

"How does one become a butterfly?"

The answer? "You must want to fly so much that you are willing to give up being a caterpillar."

I have learned that when we let go of what is no longer serving and supporting us, we make room for what will. And like the caterpillar climbing out of its cocoon, it is a worthwhile trip.

You emerge as the butterfly and get to fly to your dreams, to the success you've sabotaged until now. Climb out of your cocoon and out of the environment that has held you back. Your dreams will be there waiting for you. Open your arms. Your time is NOW.

Shannon Tobin
October 2012

The Lesson of the Butterfly

One day, a small opening appeared in a cocoon; a man sat and watched for the butterfly for several hours as it struggled to force its body through that little hole. It appeared as if it had gotten as far as it could and it could not go any further. Then, it seemed to stop making any progress. So the man decided to help the butterfly: he took a pair of scissors and opened the cocoon. The butterfly then emerged easily. But it had a withered body; it was tiny with shriveled wings.

The man continued to watch because he expected that, at any moment the wings would open, enlarge and expand, to be able to support the butterfly's body and become firm. Neither happened. In fact, the butterfly spent the rest of its life crawling around with a withered body and shriveled wings. It never was able to fly.

What the man, in his kindness and his goodwill, did not understand was that the restricting cocoon and the struggle required for the butterfly to get through the tiny opening were God's way of forcing fluid from the body of the butterfly into its wings, so that it would be ready for flight once it achieved its freedom from the cocoon.

Adapted from a story by Sonaira D'Avila

Sometimes, struggles are exactly what we need in our life. If God allowed us to go through our life without any obstacles, it would cripple us. We would not be as strong as we could have been and would ever have been able to fly.

When you ask for Strength... God will give you difficulties to make you strong.

When you ask for Wisdom... God will give you problems to solve.

When you ask for Prosperity...God will give you a brain and will power to work.

When you ask for Courage... God will give you obstacles to overcome.

When you ask for Love...God will give you troubled people to help.

When you ask for favors...God will give you opportunities. The greatest lessons are in receiving everything you don't want...but everything you need.

I challenge you to live life without fear, confront all obstacles and know that you can overcome them.

The first step to living the life you want is leaving the life you don't want. Taking the first step forward is always the hardest. But then each step forward gets you closer and closer, until eventually what had once been invisible starts to become visible. What you once felt impossible starts to feel possible.

I truly believe that the obstacles and hardships we face in life are stepping-stones to a brighter future. And also helps us empathize with others when they go through them. I also believe that God gives us the exact experiences he wants us to have in order to shape the specific destiny he's designed for us.

The best way to identify what God wants to do in your life is to hear about the discovery process in someone else's.

However, be sure the Dream in your heart is biblically based, affirmed by the balcony people in your life, and linked to your passions, gifts and life experiences.

I hope my story will inspire, move and encourage you to have audacious faith to dedicate your life to discovering your purpose and fulfilling it.

Begin today by asking God to do something seemingly impossible in your life.

Take the first step to discovering an audacious vision, by seizing God's big purpose for your life! He's waiting for you to manifest it!

CHAPTER 1

Clarity Is Power

"I was once lost but now I'm found," says it all! Up until just recently, I lived through the lenses of very foggy glasses and didn't realize the greatness that was stored within me until going through a series of painful experiences/life lessons.

It wasn't until I faced the mirror that clarity became so evident to me. It all began at a very young age when my father was tragically killed in a working accident when my twin brother and I were just about to turn three years old. That painful loss set the course of an entirely different road and future for our family.

December 2, 1973 was the day our life as a family turned a corner and went on an entirely different direction. As the years past, I began to question "why" and felt a void but couldn't put my finger on it. Back then, you didn't speak as freely and openly about those things, nor was therapy the norm as it is today.

Now I understand it fully and see that all the "not so good" tasting things that happen in life are the necessary ingredients to creating my recipe of success. Think of a chocolate chip cookie. The final product is delicious, but if you were to taste each individual ingredient it can taste a little nasty can't it? Life is no different. There are no mistakes! You may feel something isn't fair, justified or meant to happen. But hold on - the final product is just being created and put in the mixing bowl, waiting to be baked. Embrace

You owe the world your gifts. You just have to find out how to use them.

From the Amazing Spiderman

each ingredient in your life and know that God is working his magic through you as we speak! Knowing this, I can look back and see the significance behind this tragedy in our family; it was one of the 'not so great' tasting ingredients in the recipe for a greater life. It also helped shape me into the woman I am today. My mom is truly one of the strongest women I know. She not only had to go back to work in order to provide for my brother and me, but her commitment to be a rock and pillar for us was non-negotiable.

She taught us that no matter what happens in life, you keep going. Things will not always be perfect or rosy but we have two choices: to quit or persist through the pain. I'm so grateful to my mom for her strength and commitment to not become a victim of her circumstances but a victor and role model to my brother and me.

I've seen many women crumble and curl up in a ball or bury themselves and never come out when tragedy hits, but my mom leaned on her faith and pressed on even during the most difficult times. She never quit! I never thought that the choices I would make, years down the road would be a reflection of all that she taught me. However, not having a strong male role model in my life led me to make some poor choices when it came to relationships with men. Do I regret any of my choices? Absolutely not!

I believe everything happens for a reason and the people who come into our lives are there for a reason, a season or a lifetime. I also believe that when the pain of remaining the same becomes greater than the pain of change, the decisions and choices we make will change.

> Our lives are a sum total of the choices we've made. Embrace the challenges and struggles. They are a necessary ingredient for victory!
>
> Author unknown

In 2008, I realized that something needed to give! On the outside everything looked healthy, lush and perfect as though I was thriving in life, but on the inside I was dead and merely just surviving. Ironically, that was the year I led my unit to the number one position in all of Canada. Many would have loved to have been in my shoes, but what they didn't see were insides of my shoes. My soul was torn up, and needed to be mended or, better yet, replaced.

My marriage was crumbling and I was just surviving each day to the next, suffocating myself in the process, as I blanketed one problem over another. I soon, also realized that I was only in control of one person's actions...mine! You can't make someone else happy or mold them into someone they don't want to be. Nor can someone truly love another if they don't love themselves.

Far too often we travel through life on autopilot, going through the motions, accepting what is, and having every day pass like the one before it. This was becoming my life! I merely existed and felt so isolated due to the fact that I worked, and came home with very little social life outside of my career and home life. My close friends drifted away, and we sure weren't creating new friendships.

I was suddenly realizing that the void in my life was not just in the relationships outside of my marriage but also more in my marriage itself. The layers of blankets that I kept covering over one another soon suffocated me, and I couldn't breathe anymore.

I felt trapped, frustrated and the urge to break through the mold of conformity was becoming stronger and stronger every day. However, the one thing that kept holding me back was the fact that I cared more about what others thought than I did my own happiness and freedom.

What I know to be true now? It's never too late to embrace an audacious vision for your life! No matter how far behind you feel, or how many opportunities you feel you've let go, you can begin to ask God to do the Impossible in your life right now.

In October 2008, I attended a Mary Kay workshop held by my National Sales Director, and it was at that retreat that I realized I was ready to make some serious changes in myself to find my identity and take control of my life instead of continuing to allow it to control me.

Little did I know, the three-year process that I was about to embark on would give me the courage and strength to leave an unhealthy toxic marriage. My son was two years old at the time, and I felt as though the only decision I had was to "put up and shut up."

That shows you how I valued my worth, doesn't it? Love isn't supposed to hurt. And if it does, it's not true love.

At any given moment we have the power to say, "This is not how my story is going to end." That was the weekend I made the commitment to get the help I needed to begin that journey within myself. I became thirsty and passionate about discovering my identity and purpose in life. However, one thing I didn't see coming were the painful lessons I'd have to endure along the way. Every experience and decision we make, good and bad, is what molds and forms us. I became very clear that facing the mirror was the only way I was going to be able to break through this steel

> The greatest power you have in this world is the power of your own self-transformation. It starts with the one in the mirror.
>
> Shannon M. Tobin

barrier standing in the way of my greater self. The things I knew to be true: God's hands were on this the entire time and my dad was my guardian angel.

However, I wasn't able to distinguish the difference between God's path and the enemy's because I was broken, vulnerable and so desperately seeking love and approval from someone! God sends us messages, red flags and signals; however, until we're ready to receive them, we will ignore or make them appear to be reasons to move toward something instead of away.

I made the decision at that workshop to begin one-on-one coaching with the keynote speaker who attended that workshop.

What I thought was going to be a short-term coaching relationship, turned into a much deeper relationship where a line was crossed physically, mentally and emotionally.

God always had a way of protecting our journey to some degree. However, if we're not willing to see the red flags as signals to change or adjust our sails his hands are tied, and we will need to discover the painful lessons on our own. And that's exactly what happened. I saw a few red flags/warning signs at the very beginning of my coaching, but chose to ignore them and continue on. I can see God now saying: "Girl, I tried to show you and save you from the pain you were about to endure, but because you chose to ignore the red flags, you needed to experience first-hand, the message behind the mess. As soon as you chose to put me in the driver's seat, I was able to get you back on track in the direction so you could manifest your dreams."

One thing I know to be true: there are consequences to every action and decision we make, good or bad. Some of these decisions cost me greatly - financially, mentally, spiritually and emotionally. When you put more trust in someone, other than yourself, and bare your heart and soul to them, you can also become a vulnerable target.

I felt I was strong and ready to conquer the world once I discovered who I was and what I wanted and deserved in life. However, I didn't realize how co-dependent I would become in the process, which also made me an open target to being manipulated, controlled and taken advantage of.

This is exactly why so many women go from one toxic/abusive or unhealthy relationship, into another right away. Clearly, that was my case. There was not enough time, healing and proper treatment done prior to this. In fact, I went from knowing my marriage was over to crossing the line with my coach before my marriage was even dissolved. Not something I'm proud of in the least. However, the reason I am writing my story is to share my pain, mess and lessons so that I can help, inspire and encourage other women who are experiencing the same thing, or may know of someone who is, not to go down the same road I went down. I also want to put a mirror in front of every coach, leader and/or mentor out there to remind you of your code of ethics and moral responsibility when dealing with a client, especially one in a major storm or about to enter one.

It wasn't until a year and a half after my separation that my eyes were opened! Weeks of literally no returned phone calls or contact with my coach

> What you decide is where you'll abide. Stop looking back at your failures and choose to look ahead to your destiny.
>
> Shannon M. Tobin

made the red flags become even more evident. I was beginning to see that he had no intention of paying me back that last $5,400 I paid him. I felt used, abused and once again taken advantage of. He had charged me several thousand dollars for services he never delivered but, because of my loyalty to him and the fact I had fallen deeply for him, I tried to give him the benefit of the doubt, hoping and praying he would come forward and reimburse me, but that didn't happen. I didn't have the courage until almost a year later to call him on it. Goes to show you how little I valued myself. Because our relationship became more than that of coach/client, this was devastating to say the least. On the other hand, it was almost like God was putting another red flag in front of me, hoping I would see it for what it was worth this time! I decided to calculate every invoice I had paid out to him and came to find that within the first six months of my separation, he received over $20,000 of my money. I was shocked, angry and couldn't believe how I'd been blinded by love. I have a strong feeling that I'm not the only one this has happened to but no one else has had the courage or strength to speak about it. Since he continued to ignore my calls, I had no other choice than to send him an email calling him on his conduct. And when I did approach him on it, he became very defensive, angry, and tried to turn the entire blame back on me and said I was accusing him of this because our relationship went sour. There was no relationship now that I look back. It was all a long-distance fantasy that I thought would turn into a fairytale romance. Now that the foggy glasses are off, I'm sure his intention was just that. I was another one of the fish in the sea that took the bait... hook, line and sinker. But what he didn't realize was the strength behind my pain would some day be unleashed, and I would meet a mentor and coach with credibility and integrity who would encourage me to turn this mess into a message and warning signal to all the women out there who may be in the same boat, but not strong enough to stop it. This was the last straw for me, and I wasn't going to lose my power to anyone anymore! Sometimes we need to get hurt, broken into pieces and trampled on before we can see what's happening. Even though some of my dear, closest friends tried to show me the mirror, I had to come to a place of truth in order for me to see it myself. This time I wasn't going to ignore it!

Not only was I in the middle of a major storm already - getting ready to go to court with my ex husband - but now, I had to fight this emotional battle, as well. It was my worst nightmare. Or so I thought at the time. Sometimes we need to be hit with two big whammies for us to clearly see the path we're on. I went as far as doing a private investigation on my former coach to find that he had claimed bankruptcy in the past, did not own a home - as he said he did - had moved many times over the last 10 years, had several alias names and had previous leans and court orders against him. My lawyer told me that even if I did win, she couldn't guarantee I would ever see that money. You can't get blood out of a stone. I was exhausted and drained emotionally, mentally, physically and financially. So I decided to take the loss and move on. However I missed an important element and that was forgiveness. Not only was I beating myself up for allowing myself to be taken advantage of but also for not saying something when I

You cannot change the circumstances, the seasons, or the wind, but you can change yourself. That's something you have charge of.

Jim Rohn

wanted to and continuing to allow something that was not right to go on. I felt like it was déjà vu. A good friend saw me struggling with this and reassured me that the money I lost would come back to me 10 fold. Well, I was ready, willing and able to start reaping those returns.

I truly believe this was my final wake up call to get up, stand up and unleash the strong woman God created me to be. I was at my lowest of lows and had one of two decisions to make: to either pull up my big girl panties and take control or allow this to control me.

Thank God I chose to allow my audacious faith to get me through this. If I wanted to see God do something impossible in my life, I had to open my heart and mind to God's vision for my life. It started when I chose to step out in strength not my own to pursue God's larger purpose for my life. This bold act was a move of God!

I sat back and thought to myself, "How can I continue to raise my son and be a role model to the thousands of women in Mary Kay with this scarcity survival mentality?" This wake-up call became my driving force to not give up and be the change I wanted to see.

Seizing God's vision meant me deciding that I would not spend another day surviving in my dysfunctional situation.

Once I realized this I began the healing process and chose to learn from all the mistakes instead of fall victim to them. There was no way I was going to let a third man take another piece of me and destroy it. Instead I got on my knees, surrendered and put God in the driver's seat!

My former coach might have been successful at getting my trust and money, but there was no way

I was going to allow him to control my resilience to get back up and keep going.

Now that I look back at this four-year journey of tough lessons, I wouldn't change a thing. I've become wiser and stronger for it and realize the importance of putting God in the driver's seat and listening to my gut and intuition.

It has to be an all or nothing commitment. When you're only 99 percent in, you're 100 percent out! Now that I've chosen to trust God's path 100 percent, I don't question the path. Nor do I sweat the small stuff like I used to. I can now laugh at things that used to rock me or take me out of my game. It's a great feeling when you can see the light at the end of the tunnel.

Faith is to believe what you do not see. The reward of Faith is to see what you've always believed, according to Saint. Augustine.

Notes

CHAPTER 2

Healing You

We're either in a crisis, on our way out of a crisis or entering into a crisis. This is life! A crisis usually hits when we least expect it and will rock us and test our strength. We can either react or respond to a crisis and fall victim to it or choose to become a victor over the circumstance.

So often, I see women quit, give up, crumble and break into pieces while in crisis or a storm. What kept me from entering that mindset? My faith was number one, my family number two and my career number three.

I knew that if God led me to it, he would help me through it. I asked him to open the exit door for me, and he did. That was a sign that I just needed to keep the faith in Him and lean on Him even that much more.

My son Cole was, and always will be my "WHY!" and the number one reason I press forward when being rocked, knocked down or disappointed. If I crumbled and fell apart, what lessons would I be teaching him? I'm not saying that he didn't see me cry or feel the effects of the divorce. However, what was more important for me to let him see was how I managed in the midst of the storm. Life will always throw us curve balls and challenges, but how we respond or react will determine the outcome and whether we have a victim mentality or victor mentality. I want Cole to see that with God, we can weather any storm. We became that much more dedicated to God's

Some people are going to get the shock of their lives when they see that you didn't just survive without them, you thrived.

Shannon M. Tobin

God gave us wings, like eagles, to rise above our circumstances, to manifest our greatness with purpose and intention.

Shannon M. Tobin

hand leading us, found a church and a new-found faith. He witnessed me give my life 100 percent to Jesus as I was baptized just two weeks after we started attending church. This was a miracle in itself. Letting go of the past in order to embrace the future was my new resolution and commitment to not only me but to God. This was very personal between God and me, and he was the only one whose presence mattered.

As a leader, trainer and mentor in Mary Kay, I not only had an obligation but a duty to fulfill and live. I was already under a microscope, being watched, admired and emulated by so many. The thought of letting the sales force down, my sister Mary Kay Directors and Consultants, made me nauseous. How could I tell them to persevere, have faith and never give up, if I wasn't willing to? Leadership credibility has always been important to me, and I wasn't about to let that slide because of my insecurities and fears.

When you discover God's calling and purpose for your life, you must be willing to risk a season of pain to create a life of gain. I had more than a season, but when I think of the gain, it was worth every scar that eventually led me to my place of freedom - freedom to be, do, have, live and give! You can't give what you do not have. However, the more you give, the more you will receive. So, instead of focusing on the challenges, obstacles and problems, I chose to focus on the gifts and blessings in my life and I began to receive more of them.

They say your children are a reflection of you and it's up to us what kind of legacy we will leave behind for them. Sometimes it's easier said than done. Until you are hit with something you are willing to take action on, nothing will change. I began to see the effects of what an unhealthy relationship/marriage was doing to my son, and a paradigm shift took place. Staying married for the sake of your child is not always the best thing to do, especially if they don't see love, commitment and loyalty in that marriage. The last thing I would ever want would be for my son to grow up thinking that this was ok and how a relationship should look. Our children will become the product of what they see, and the more dysfunction they are exposed to and experience will be carried through their entire lives. So in January 2010, I made the decision to end my marriage. I let go of being so concerned about what other people were going to think and put my son and myself in first priority. I stopped covering up the real issue with a Band-Aid hoping it would go away. I'm so thankful that I saw this when my son was still young enough to not be scarred for life.

Ending my marriage was probably the most difficult thing I had to do at that time in my life! When you've allowed someone to be co-dependent on you for so long, yet controlling at the same time, you carry a lot of guilt, anger and resentment. Do I blame it all on him? Absolutely not! I had to forgive myself for allowing it to go on for so long. It showed how weak I was and how little I valued my own worth to be.

Divorce isn't easy but sometimes it's the best thing for all parties. Now that I look back almost three years later, I see things in an entirely different light with my eyes, wide open. During my marriage, God wasn't part of the picture. I had a faith but wasn't courageous and bold enough to live it out loud. And attending church would have meant doing it alone and I wasn't ready, nor did I want to add that to the list of battles I was already fighting. Now that the foggy glasses have been removed I see how controlled I was and this was yet another thing I chose to conform to.

We are where we are "today" based on the choices we've made, or have allowed someone else to make for us. I was constantly beating myself over the head with a club instead of seeing that there were other choices.

One of the greatest challenges in life is being yourself in a world that's trying to make you like everyone else. I began to see that I didn't have to settle anymore, and that it was a choice I was making for myself, not someone else making for me. To become bold enough and do for me instead of always caring so much about what others thought. Once I broke the mold of conformity, it soon became a new mission, not only be true to myself but to empower others to do the same.

Following your dream and purpose, no matter what others think or say, is so vitally important to move from surviving to thriving in life. Most go without and do things just to please others versus living their passion and doing what's important to them. It's been said that the majority of people in the world today are just surviving and 68 percent of people truly believe that they've already lived their best years.

I believe I've got a new lease on life and am just now beginning to LIVE the life that God had pre-destined for me!

The only way I was able to find my true passion and discover what made my heart sing, was to face the dreaded mirror and begin to peel back the onion one layer at a time. This wasn't an overnight

Often, God makes a move after we make a move. He directs our steps, but we have to step out in faith.

Victoria Osteen

process; however, with each new day and each layer it became easier as I began to see the changes manifest in me. I was discovering what happiness and inner peace and strength really felt like, in amongst the ring of fire (as I described it) and that gave me the courage and desire to keep going.

There is no greater feeling than blasting through that ring of fire as a new woman, at last living each day in my purpose, truly able to see my gifts and confident to stand in my power for the very first time in my life!

On my 41st birthday, I owned my personal power for the first time! I couldn't understand at the time why it had to happen on my birthday, but after that day it became evident to me. To finally have the courage and strength to be bold enough and stand in front of the courts, speaking my truth with strength and confidence was empowering and liberating! I was able to stand up and tell my side of the story, not my attorney, when my ex-husband and I were in divorce court on that day.

Until you can look in the mirror and love yourself from the inside out, you will never be able to speak your truth and love others the way God wants you to.

It wasn't until I had made a decision that it was God's path or nothing, that the transformation really became evident and in motion. All it took was taking myself out of the driver's seat and putting God in it each and every day. Sounds simple doesn't it? I always thought that "I" needed to be in control and take the responsibility for the outcome but until I released that, I continued to spin my wheels in frustration while going nowhere. It's such a great feeling to be in the passenger seat with him behind the wheel navigating the path I need to be on and making the adjustments and knowing which detour or road to take. Sometimes it means going against the status quo and choosing to take a road less travelled. Something I was uncomfortable doing before, until I stepped over the line.

When I look back, I know that every single challenge, obstacle and pain I endured was for a purpose and specific lesson!

It wasn't until then, that I was truly able to see my place in this world. I knew why God created me and that my purpose on this earth was to help others break through the mold of conformity, to see their true beauty hidden deep beneath all of their pain.

This is what it means to seize your vision and become significant versus successful. What the scoreboard says means nothing unless you are living a Godly life helping others manifest their God-given talents and abilities. By becoming real and transparent through sharing my journey, I'm now able to be a beacon of light for someone else.

I truly believe the lessons, hardships, and pain we experience along the way are given to us so we can help someone else navigate and stay strong during their storm.

For God has not given us a spirit of fear, but of power, love and sound mind.

1 Timothy 1:7 NKJV

Notes

CHAPTER 3

Success Is An Inside Job

When I look back over the 20 years of building my business, and think about all the ingredients I've tasted along the way, there were a few specific ones that helped shape me into the person I am today.

Let me go back to when I was a child. Every child experiences the cruel behavior that takes place during adolescent years. And many of those painful experiences are carried into our adulthood, however, they don't surface until several years later, usually when we hit a wall or stop growing and have to look in the mirror to discover what's holding us back. Even though I had the external look of confidence, my inner self worth and self esteem was lacking in a big way, which in the end, was a big hurdle that I needed to face.

I initially grew my business on the mentality of: Effort = Results and felt that if I never gave up, I would ultimately reach the pinnacle of success in Mary Kay and drive the trophy on wheels…the pink Cadillac. Yes, that was true but I often found myself constantly focused on what the scoreboard said, versus being driven by a mission and running my own race. Once I "got it", I saw the true value in not comparing myself to others. These lessons became the driving force that took me from where I was, to where I wanted to be. I'm sure you can relate to this when I say I was stuck, and tired of being sick and tired.

Every glory has a story. Until you discover who you are, you'll never realize the stuff you're made of.

Shannon M. Tobin

Once I reached a management level in my business, I coasted for several years, working hard but dedicated to discipline only. It's best to say I wasn't purpose-driven, working for a cause greater than myself. It was killing me trying to figure out what I needed to get fixed or change in order for me to take my business from that level to the level of a Top Director. At the time, I didn't realize it had nothing to do with my skill set, but everything to do with my mentality?

I was self-sabotaging and didn't realize it. This self-sabotage was mainly because of a scar that was formed in my early years of grade school. I was a typical little girl, slightly chubby and definitely not the smartest in the class. Typical of playground behavior, one day I'd have all the friends in the world at school, and the next day I would have none or few. It only took one ringleader to form the group, and everyone followed her lead. Today they would call it bullying, but back then it just looked like a popularity contest. As a result, because I lacked self-esteem, I was clearly not a leader back then but a follower.

I soon conformed to the game, and my mentality became one of insecurity and conformity. I wasn't aware of it, so I carried that baggage into my high school years and into my business life as a young adult.

Because I didn't see and value my worth, I wasn't able to look into a mirror and see my inner beauty and strength. All I saw were the visible flaws from an external view, which I didn't like. I became obsessed with becoming thin, all to get the attention of a boy. Eating healthy and exercising weren't working fast enough for me, so the only other alternative was to turn to purging after

When your 'why' becomes clear, the how will appear.

Shannon M. Tobin

each and every meal. It became an obsession and an addiction. It got to the point where I didn't even have to think about it anymore, it had become a daily habit. What I didn't know was that a friend, who also purging, became aware and pointed it out to me while we were at a Catholic weekend retreat. God was working behind the scene big time, and it was there that we made a pact that we would no longer continue this unhealthy road. I thank God as I know that it was through "his" intervention, while at that retreat, that I was able to quit that quickly. Sadly, many don't have the strength, courage or ability to just say enough is enough; I'm done with this! The blessing in all of this is that because I've been through it, I can relate to someone else and possibly give them the hope to make a decision to get the help they need. Another mess I can turn into a message.

Empowering children to develop self-confidence, and self-esteem has become a passion of mine! This is a missing link in today's society because parents are so busy, overworked and running around with their children in their extra-curricular activities that the one-on-one connection is no longer there.

Because of this, I've chosen not to get caught up in that race and put parenting as my number one objective. My job as Cole's mom is to build a healthy foundation for him, empower him to see his strengths and to have him working for a cause.

Think about this: What is your why and purpose driven mission in life?

The definition of insanity is doing the same thing over and over again but expecting different results. The number one thing holding me

We are all born with a script. Your past has no significance for your future as soon as you fire the editor of your past.

Author unknown

God grant me
the serenity
to accept the
things I cannot
change;
courage to
change the
things I can;
and wisdom
to know the
difference.

The Serenity Prayer

back from success was me and my lack of self-worth until one day, early in my career, God put Independent National Sales Director Bernice Boe Malin into my space, not just for a reason, season but for a lifetime. She is a woman who is a master at affirming others' greatness. She taught me the importance of breathing belief into people through her notes, words and actions. All it took was to have her say, "Shannon, we've been waiting for you girl! You've got to join us on the top trip next year to Vienna. It's time you joined the big girls club." Wow! How powerful, and simple to do! She elevated me to a whole new 'deserve' level, and I am forever grateful to her for that.

Pleasantly surprised and greatly inspired, that conversation changed the trajectory of my business. That next year, I took my business from the $350,000 unit club to the $650,000.

Not because I learned a new skill, but because of a mentality shift. For the first time, I felt I belonged and fit in. I know I'm not the only one that has ever felt like this. So often I see women struggling, looking for the magic bullet or secret to success, and they continually try to tweak their performance versus digging deep and discovering the real issue behind the pain of their performance.

It only took one person who was where I wanted to be to accept me into the group and give me the reassurance I belonged there. I know I'm not alone and more women are fighting the acceptance battle.

I am now committed to do the same for others.

One thing I know to be true: your words will either elevate someone or tear them down. I think we need to experience both in order to come to the realization of how we want to be treated and how to treat others.

The next incident wasn't so uplifting. In fact it was the exact opposite. I was a Cadillac director and had earned an invitation to a Mary Kay gala dinner at one of the leadership conferences. I couldn't tell you which one it was, but I can tell you of the incident that feels as real and vivid today as it was 13 or so years ago.

This gala was filled with top achievers including all the Independent National Sales Directors, who were attending that specific conference. I wanted to have my photo taken with as many of these top achievers as I could so I could put them on my vision board, as they were where I wanted to be.

It doesn't matter how many times I tell this story, it still chokes me up and hits a chord. I walked up to one of the Independent National Sales Directors and asked her if I could have my picture taken with her. She looked me straight in the eye and said very bluntly, "I don't have time," and walked away.

I was shocked, crushed, embarrassed, humiliated, hurt and wanted to dig myself a hole and crawl into it. Unfortunately, due to my lack of self-worth, I allowed her actions to ruin my entire evening. I remember lying in bed that evening asking God for the lesson behind this pain, and he answered with this: "Now you know how *not* to treat someone." I remembered reading a quote from John C Maxwell that read: "Hurting people hurt people." I soon came to the realization that her words and actions had nothing to do with me. This experience has helped me over the years in more ways than one. I've been able to share my story and empathize with others because of what I'd experienced.

From that day forward, I promised myself that I would never allow success or status to go to my head and to always make the time, no matter how busy I was, to give someone a few minutes of my time. Mary Kay Ash used to say: "Pretend that everyone we meet is wearing a sign around their neck that says, 'Make me feel important.'" I'm far from perfect, but one thing I know for sure, I'm committed to do everything in my power to add value to the people I meet. A simple word of encouragement can be just what that person needed to carry on through the day and keep going.

I'm so thankful for these two lessons, as they played a huge part of my personal journey and became the steppingstones for discovering God's purpose for me.

Two things I know to be true:

1. How someone treats you (good or bad) is a direct reflection of them, not you.

And

2. Hurting people hurt people.

Over the years, I've come to realize that the biggest lessons I've learned have come with a price, a hefty price with much pain! It's during the storms that we sometimes fail to see the lessons and reasoning behind why something is taking place.

But I do have to say that once I embraced the path and truly let go and let God, the challenges didn't seem as big, and I felt more at ease with the process. I learned to "go with the flow" more and not "sweat the small stuff!"

> Allow people the grace to change because you will need that same grace one day after you've made a mistake.
>
> Tony Gaskins Jr

It's not about me anymore! Believing God for the impossible and understanding what He wants to accomplish through me is now my new focus and passion! When you become others-focused and help someone find their need, miraculous things begin to happen - not only them, but for you as well. A win/win!

I also believe that we are where we are today based on the choices we've made or have allowed others to make for us. I'm not saying we can control what others do and say, however, we can choose whether we respond or react to what they do and say. We are 100 percent in control of our thoughts and actions. How we choose to respond or react to the challenges we're faced, will determine our outcome.

I was a reactor for many years, constantly feeling the need to defend myself. Maybe that was my way of protecting my outer shell from getting cracked. Or, now as I look back, it spoke volumes about the fact that I was hurt and deeply scarred. In the long run, this caused me more heartaches and damage than it did good. When you're in a battle with yourself and not being true to who you are, it doesn't matter what others do or say to try and help you, you will always react in a negative way and become defensive.

When I discovered who Shannon Tobin is, I began to break that mold. My performance changed, along with my circle of influence. I began to realize that some of the people I allowed into my small circle would wind up hurting me deeply, breaking my trust and putting me back in defense mode. Call it naïve; call it weak; call it what you will. I would rather chalk it up to it being just another lesson that I needed to learn along my journey of discovering God's purpose for my life!

I can look back now and appreciate the fact that people come into your life for a reason, a season or a lifetime. When you know which one it is, you will know what to do for that person - either hang on and embrace them or let go and release them.

It was during the storm, that this poem came across my desk. A message sent to me that eased my pain and brought me great peace:

"When someone is in your life for a reason, it is usually to meet a need you have expressed. They have come to assist you through a difficulty, to provide you with guidance and support, to aid you physically, emotionally or spiritually. They may seem like a godsend and they are. They are there for the reason you need them to be. Then, without any wrongdoing on your part or at an inconvenient time, this person will say or do something to bring the relationship to an end.

Sometimes they die. Sometimes they walk away. Sometimes they act up and force you to take a stand. What we must realize is that our need has been met, our desire fulfilled, their work is done. The prayer you sent up has been answered and now it is time to move on.

Some people come into your life for a season, because your turn has come to share, grow or learn. They bring you an experience of peace or make you laugh. They may teach you something you have never done. They usually give you an unbelievable amount of joy. Believe it, it is real. But only for a season.

> Let your purpose define you, not your hardships. Remember, a diamond started out as a lump of coal. Allow God to mold you through the pressure.
>
> Author unknown

Lifetime relationships teach you lifetime lessons, things you must build upon in order to have a solid emotional foundation. Your job is to accept the lesson, love the person and put what you have learned to use in all other relationships and areas of your life."

--Author unknown

Maya Angelou once said: "When people show you who they are, believe them."

It wasn't until I truly understood this that I was able to begin my healing process. But one thing had to happen first.... forgiving myself.

Forgiving myself for falling for manipulation; forgiving myself for allowing myself to be deceived; forgive myself for staying and putting up with the verbal and emotional abuse; forgiving myself for ignoring the red flags. Once I forgave myself, I was able to love myself enough to say, "It's okay, there's a lesson to be learned here."

Once I was able to let go and forgive myself, I was able to see the lessons from the broken pieces and was no longer going to fight against my destiny. That became my new focus, purpose and passion. I knew that if I was going through this, someone else surely was too, and that my story may be an inspiration to someone else.

Notes

CHAPTER 4

Discovering Your Occupassion

If I could choose one word to define myself today, it would be passion.

It's a passion for God, life, work, family, friends and, most of all, freedom! It's a true, undying kind of passion that hasn't been taught and learned, but rather formed deep within the crevices of my heart through my lifelong experiences.

My 20-year journey to this point all began with the search for personal growth – the kind that would land me a dream job in my field of architecture and interior design. Little did I know that what would start as a step towards self-improvement would become a dream lifestyle full of harmony.

It all began with my mom, who recently celebrated her 29th anniversary with Mary Kay. My mom embraced the Mary Kay opportunity, making it the vehicle that would provide a lifestyle many just dream about for me and my twin brother Sean. My mom was able to provide for us financially and be there for us physically and emotionally. That's not always possible for a single mother. She adopted an 'others-focused' mentality for us, and, through this experience, I am now able to do the same for my own son.

Today, I'm grateful for my Mary Kay business and all the blessings that have come from my commitment and willingness to work, risk and sacrifice. It is a lifestyle to which I can't attach a price tag.

Have a passion for a cause, for what you do, for what you are, for what you stand for! Most importantly, live today as if it's your last!

Author unknown

There's a difference between interest and commitment. When you're interested in doing something, you do it only when it's convenient. When you're committed to something, you accept no excuses, only results. We can also use our children as an excuse or a reason to press on, take a stand and overcome obstacles in the face of adversity.

Mary Kay is the best-kept secret out there for women. It's a hidden treasure for which many women search. Yes, there are other great jobs, but Mary Kay Ash, the woman, didn't create them. That's the difference! Mary Kay overcame so many hardships to form a vision so clear, so big. She was 'others-focused' and quitting was never an option. I admired her for her tenacity and willingness to take a stand for what she believed in – never compromising her ethics and integrity.

This is a legacy that I'm committed to passing on to others, and it warms my heart when my unit members catch the same vision and pass on the Mary Kay values to others.

> If you want God to do something impossible in your life, you've got to open your heart and mind to God's vision for your life.
>
> Steven Furtick

When I changed my thinking, I changed my life

Initially, when I walked into the front door of my Mary Kay business, I locked the back door and threw away the key. Sitting on the fence is a painful place. Not only does it paralyze you, but others as well. No one wants to follow a parked car.

Too many people have the mentality that they'll try the business for six months and if it doesn't work, they'll quit. That wasn't an option for me.

Was it easy? No. Did I earn the use of a Cadillac right away? No. However, I rose above the naysayers and knew I could only count on one person...ME! I went to every event and function and attending weekly meetings was non-negotiable – I showed up, I plugged in and had great mentors along the way.

Faith, family, career. In this order, everything works; out of this order, nothing works.

If you are to succeed, you must understand that your rewards in life will be in direct proportion to the contribution you make. When you fully grasp this principle, apply it to your work; you will have little concern over money again. Apply it to your personal and professional relationships, and you'll be overwhelmed with the love and admiration you receive from others.

From the book *Sun Stand Still*: "What we call a miracle is really just the right combination of your ordinary ingredients and God's ordinary expertise. And when God's super collides with your natural, sparks will fly."

Here's an example: God may lead you to stay home with your young children, forfeiting a second income – ordinary. But along with diapers, dishes, and naps, you receive the gift of time to model discipline, instill values and speak life into your kids. They grow up to be Joshua's in their own generation – extraordinary!

Look around your desert today. It might be your office, your living room, your church, your neighborhood or your classroom. If God is calling you to make a difference, he usually starts in a small way. Your flaming bush may appear as a tiny spark that only you will notice.

Will you remove your shoes, draw close and receive your assignment? Will you give the Lord permission to ignite your ordinary? If you will, I

It's time to stop raising our kids to survive in the world and start empowering them with a vision to change it.

Steven Furtick

promise it won't be long before your faith starts carrying you to a level higher than you ever thought you could go.

Thank you Independent National Sales Director Scarlett Walker-Simpson for introducing me to the book Sun Stand Still written by Steven Furtick. This book has been life changing!

When I realized I couldn't do this alone and understood the importance of putting God in the driver's seat, I gave my path over to him 100 percent.

Cole and I have this little visual of God doing the antsy dance up in heaven every time we try and solve our problems on our own. We've come to realize it's so much easier when we give it over to Him. We say daily: "God we give you this day."

One day as we were walking to the school bus, Cole said, "God I give you this world." I asked, "Why are you giving him the world instead of the day, as we normally do?" He said, "I want God to take care of everyone in the world's problems, not just ours mom." Those truly made my heart sing and confirmed to me that the gift of time I've given my son by modeling discipline, instilling values and speaking into his life is paying off.

As we labor with excellence, our children will observe the works of our God and truly see what He looks like. He will stir up your spirit, pour out His presence and reveal His glory in your family, business and community. This is the kind of faith that doesn't just change you, but also enables you to be part of a changing world.

Growing up in the Mary Kay culture gave our family many advantages. Not only did the culture teach us to dream big, but it taught us that you'll reap the rewards of hard work and dedication.

And it gave us a perspective of life in a much bigger way: struggles are a necessity for growth and anything is possible if you believe. We experienced, first hand, a mom who didn't always reach her goals when planned, but never gave up until her race was won. Most importantly, we had a mom who was there physically and emotionally when we needed her.

I heard once that little kids get into little trouble and big kids get into big trouble. That statement is true if a parent is absent, but my mom made a point to be there every morning before we went off to school and was there to greet us every day after school. She was the mom a lot of our childhood friends wish they had so our house became a popular hangout place. I didn't realize the value in all of that or how special that was until years later as I look back now as a single mom and entrepreneur.

I thank my mom every day for her work ethic and determination to give my brother and me a better life. Not only did she lead us by example but showed us the importance of living a life of significance. We didn't always have the best of the best in material things, but we did have the best of the best when it came to a loving mom and role model.

My brother Sean has been one of my greatest cheerleaders. I'm so grateful for his love, friendship and support. I'm so proud of the man he's become, a successful Naval Architect, working for the National Defense and currently designing the next war ship. He's also just received a very prestigious award for his hard work and dedication in this project. He and his wife, Asami, are amazing parents to their two children, Ayame and Kevin.

When you make up your mind that 'the best' is the only thing you will accept, everything else that is less than the best will be eliminated.

Author unknown

The sweetest

satisfaction lies

not in climbing

your own Mount

Everest, but in

helping others

climb theirs.

Paul Thurston

When you love what you do, you'll never work another day in your life! I truly believe this and feel so blessed to lead the most amazing group of women who span all across Canada, the U.S., Portugal and India. Women who have embraced Mary Kay's vision to enrich our lives by helping us see our God-given talents and abilities. The best gift we can give through what we do is not just a great product, but more importantly, the gift of hope! When you become 'others focused' and help someone find their need and show them how Mary Kay can be the vehicle to fill it, everyone benefits. That's a win/win in life!

It's all about seizing God's vision for us! This means deciding that you will not spend another day surviving, but instead thriving. It has everything to do with you and your vision first. If you want to see God do something impossible in your life, you've got to open your heart and mind to God's vision for your life. Audacious faith starts when you choose to step out in strength, not your own, as you pursue God's larger purpose for your life. And when you act boldly, you'll find yourself in the middle of a God-inspired moment of power.

Before you can effect change in the world, you have to seize God's vision, activate your faith and then you'll make the move.

I'm dedicated to perpetuating this unique way of living to every woman who crosses my path. Showing them that they too can have whatever they want without compromising their values in the process. We're building a national area with strong Independent Beauty Consultants and Independent Sales Directors who want to be a part of something bigger.

And with the passion, persistence and positive attitude that is legendary of Mary Kay Ash, there's no doubt that we will become a Global National Area.

To me, it's not about striving for balance, but finding harmony and learning how to mesh it all together, while keeping our priorities of God, Family and Career in order...that's the key to living a life of significance and substance.

Initially, I made the decision to start my Mary Kay business for personal growth, as I lacked the self-confidence needed to land my dream job. After graduating with honors in architectural and interior design, I realized I wasn't ready to enter the working world quite yet, so I decided to give this a try for a year. My Mary Kay business became a lifelong passion and lifestyle, which has blessed me with a six-figure income for 12 consecutive years, earning over $1.3 million in commissions.

I don't say that to impress you, but to impress upon you that if I can do this, you can too. I would never have known that this was for me, unless I gave it a try. I committed to doing this for a year and then making a decision after that, whether I wanted to continue or find a job in the field in which I had a degree. As you can see, this became my occupassion and I've never looked back.

I truly believe that when you treat your business with the same respect you would another job, you will be successful. Be an "I'm glad I did" person instead of following along with the majority of the world who say "I wish I had."

Hitching my wagon to stars was something I understood to be of value and essential to the growth of my business. Because of my willingness and unwavering commitment, I promoted myself

> If you want the best the world has to offer, offer the world your best! Make 'excellence' your daily intention in all areas of your life.
>
> Shannon M. Tobin

When you become 'others' focused and help enough people get what they want, you'll get what you want.

Shannon M. Tobin

to the position of Director within 18 months of joining and have earned a total of 10 career cars, seven of them being the prestigious pink Cadillac. I've proudly represented my unit in the Top Ten 10 times, twice as many as the number-two Sales Director, and at Seminar 2009, we were number one in all of Canada. I say "we" because it was a team effort. Every single woman in my unit plays a significant role in the success of our team. No matter how much or little each contributes, it makes a difference, and I'm grateful for each and every one of them.

Because of my unwavering belief in this opportunity – combined with the hard work and dedication of our team - I've had the privilege of travelling the world on the Top Director Trips to Hong Kong, Greece, Vienna, Thailand, the Mediterranean, Switzerland, Maui, Madrid and, this year, Monaco.

I am most proud of being able to look in the mirror and be proud of who I see, confident that I can raise Cole to never give up and follow his dream. I'm also proud to be able to pass this confidence on to other women and their families, too. These factors make it worth all the sacrifices that come with my choice to become an entrepreneur.

When people ask me how was someone with so little self-confidence and self-esteem able to go from not being able to talk in front people at all to speaking to crowds of up to three thousand, I would have to say this: I learned how to fake confidence once I threw out the key to the back door and became 100 percent committed to achieving my dreams.

We are in an "events-based business" and I stand firm on the fact that it's not so much what you learn when you attend a workshop, event or seminar, but how you feel and the internal shifts that take place while you're there in the presence of powerful people. I know for a fact that my success was a result of attending an event within my first two months of being in the business. I watched ordinary women do extra ordinary things and thought, "If they can do it, so could I." I was capable and willing to give this my 100 percent and bring others on this journey with me. I became 'others focused' and committed to attending every workshop, seminar and company event so I could pass on the knowledge that I learned and lead my team by example. Dreams aren't discovered sitting at home or doing it alone.

I will be forever grateful for the lifelong lessons my Mary Kay career has taught me, which I'm paying forward to my son and all the women with whom I'm blessed to be associated.

I believe every woman deserves and needs to experience some form of Mary Kay in their life, whether it is as a customer or consultant. This opportunity is the best-kept secret, and I want the world to know about it.

We have 10 percent of the market, which means out of 10 women using some form of cosmetics, only one is using Mary Kay. That means nine out of 10 women are using the wrong products! No, seriously, this just tells me that we have an untapped market to build and need more consultants spreading the word and sharing this amazing product.

Helping women discover their God-given talents and abilities is what it's all about. The more women you help get what they want, the more you will receive. I truly believe that what we put into the lives of others will come back to us ten-fold; this means good and bad, by the way.

When my purpose became greater than my fears and challenges, I chose not to allow the ob-stacles, roadblocks, detours and negative people stop me, but instead rose above them and kept going! The pain of remaining the same was so much greater than the pain of making the chang-es. This was a mountain mover for me.

Did I do it alone? Absolutely not. I've had phe-nomenal mentors and coaches over the years, who were able to help me face the mirror, dig deep and discover my greatness. Did it come with a price? Yes! The price to work, risk and sacrifice! I had to learn to let go of the bad in order to make room for the great to enter my life.

My mom led the way by embracing her purpose of giving me and my brother a better life, which wouldn't have been possible if my Independent National Sales Director Heather Armstrong hadn't come into our lives 29 years ago. This wom-an saw something in my mom that she wasn't able to see in herself. She poured unconditional love into our family, as well as into the lives of thou-sands of women all over the world.

The song "In the Shadow of an Angel," per-formed by one of Canada's greatest singing trea-sures, Michael Ciuffo, depicts the love, apprecia-tion and gratitude I have for Heather.

Two of my biggest supporters, Heather and my mom, stood beside me, but also knew when to allow me to walk alone. This helped shape and mold me, while forming the audacious vision for my life.

The only thing you'll ever be able to take with you is the love you've given and received back in life.

Author unknown

How do you step into your personal power to create your best life?

1. If you're going to ask God to do something impossible in your life, you've got to have some clarity about what you're asking for. Be sure your dream is biblically-based, affirmed by the key people in your life and tied into your passions, gifts and life experiences.

2. Make a list of 30 reasons why you want what you want. Look at that list every day and visualize it. Revisiting that list keeps you committed and moving forward.

3. Once you've decided what it is you don't want - you'll discover what it is you do want. And then develop the skills and mindset needed to make your vision a reality. Success is an inside job! While change can be very difficult, it comes easy when you understand the process.

4. "Faith it 'til you make it" and "act" the part before you "Become the part." By doing this, you'll walk and talk with more confidence and others will want to join you on your journey.

5. Have a bounce-back mentality. If you fall, get back up again. We grow the most when being challenged or knocked down. Think bigger for you and your family than ever before. Embrace failure and know that it's essential for success, and teach others the same principles. Say: "I'm never down; I'm either up or getting back up!"

6. Remember Mary Kay Ash's advice, "For every failure, there's an alternate course of action. You just have to find it. When you come to a roadblock, take a detour."

> Passion has the power to literally transform you! Be driven by your mission.
>
> Shannon M. Tobin

No one likes to fail...no one wants to fail...but without being willing to fail... you just can't accomplish much.

David Dean

7. Success doesn't just happen. It can be painful. But ask yourself if it's more painful to remain the same. When the pain of remaining the same becomes greater than the pain of change, you will move forward.

8. Don't let the actions and opinions of those who don't matter hold you back or influence your decisions. The smaller your circle of influence the better. Remember that we become like the five people we surround ourselves with.

9. Remember that if you help enough people get what they want, you will get what you want.

10. Make a decision to act on your dreams instead of being a daydreamer. Others are watching you! You'll either be the light or darkness to someone else.

11. Always remember that pain is temporary; glory is forever! Push through the difficult times with power and purpose, and the rewards will be worth all the pain you'll endure.

12. Commit to lifelong learning. The books I've read and many of the speaker's I've listened to, have impacted my life and played a huge role in molding me into the woman I am today.

13. Be bold with your actions; live out loud, and be the best "you" each and every day. Nothing more, nothing less.

14. Run your own race and never compare yourself to others. When you do, you're comparing your worst to someone else's best.

Make a life plan list:

CHAPTER 5

Growth Comes
With A Price

As a result of losing faith and trust, I chose to stand on my own, learn on my own and truly discover who I was on my own this last year, or should I say, me, myself and God! A personal journey that I now know was a miraculous intervention from God, one that changed the trajectory of my path in more ways than one.

My solo journey was for a reason and season, which enabled me to become this strong, powerful, and purpose driven woman, who was ready to take on the world and elevate my business and life's purpose to a whole new level.

I pulled out "The Prayer of Jabez" and began to read it again faithfully every day.

It reads: "Oh, that You would bless me indeed and enlarge my territory, that Your hand would be with me, and You would keep me from evil, that I may not cause pain!"—1 Chronicles 4:10 (NKJV).

This became my daily prayer, as I felt the urgent request for these four things:

1. God's blessings. Asking God for His grace.

2. An expansion of territory. Praying for victory and prosperity in all my endeavors and that my life would be marked by increase.

3. The presence of God's hand. Asking for the guidance of God and His strength to be evident in my daily existence.

When we can't piece together the puzzle of our own lives, remember the best view of a puzzle is from above. Let God help put you together.

Amethyst Snow-Rivers

4.   Protection from harm. Looking to God in confidence as my defender.

My prayers were answered in more than one way.

There are no coincidences in life, only Godcidences! And as a result, Gary Baker re surfaced into my life. His daughter Diane and I have known each other for years and I started attending the same church as he. Gary is one of my guardian angels sent from above. He not only became a spiritual mentor to me by bringing me closer to God, but helped shape and molds me to be a disciple of Jesus and servant/leader to others. He's also been a blessing and wonderful male role model to Cole, who loves and adores him as a grandfather. A gift I couldn't put a price tag on and will cherish for life!

Another divine appointment happened in February 2012. I was introduced to a book written by author and life coach, Tony Gaskins Jr. Once again, this put me on a whole new path and journey of discovery. The book "Mrs. Right" seemed to be just what the doctor ordered and was put in my path for a specific reason: to help me see and discover my worth by taking a stand to never allow myself to be manipulated, controlled or taken advantage of ever again.

I swear that book was written just for me. Whether you are single, married, widowed or divorced, this book is a must-read for every woman, especially the young ladies entering the dating world. I believe if that book came into my life before I started to date, my journey would be different today.

I'm a firm believer that if you want something, you have to reach out and grab it. Within a couple

> Being able to move from surviving to thriving is dependent on retraining our thoughts from being mediocre to passionate.
>
> Shannon M. Tobin

weeks of reading Mrs. Right, I felt the need to reach out and ask Tony if he was taking on any more coaching clients. I never thought that sending him an email would result in him becoming my life coach but it did. It was a cosmic collision for sure!

I've always seen tremendous value in having powerful people in my circle of influence. We set up a 30-minute call, which solidified my decision to hire him on for a 3 month trial basis. Why him? He has an unwavering passion and desire to want to give back and pay it forward.

If I could choose a term to define Tony Gaskins Jr., it would be servant/ leader. Tony goes beyond self-help to total self-transformation - in mind, body and spirit - assisting others in their quest to keep God at the center of all that they do.

And as a result, I've become even more passionate and committed to leave a mark of significance on the world by fulfilling God's vision for my life. Tony helped me expand my brand and showed me the importance of giving "all" women hope, not just the women in the Mary Kay organization. This gave me the courage to take the necessary steps to begin the process of turning my mess and turn it into a message. All because I listened and followed God's path for me. I feel truly honored and blessed to be able to say I'm now an author and speaker.

Here's another example of one of God's miraculous interventions.

I've always wanted to be significant in Mary Kay, but it wasn't until I broke through my own belief barriers that I could see more for my life! The passion to help women inside and outside of Mary Kay became a burning desire. I truly believe

You don't have

to settle, it's

simply a choice

you make every

day. It's time to

reclaim your life!

Author unknown

God puts us through lessons, so we can help others who are going through what we've just experienced. You can't empathize and truly put yourself in someone else's shoes unless you've worn them first. For this reason, I have a new-found sense of purpose. I'm now driven by a bigger mission and a cause greater than myself.

To become an author and speaker has truly been a divine appointment from God. I chose to listen to his whispers this time and not sit back and say "if only" or "maybe someday." Instead, I'm embracing this next chapter of my life with open arms and audacious faith!

I want to teach women the importance of choosing a lifestyle over a job and connecting to a purpose. When you love what you do, you'll never work another day in your life. That's a saying that I believe because I'm living a lifestyle most just dream about and want each woman and man who read this to know that they too can do the same.

Life is too short, and we only go around this world once. To say "I'm glad I did vs. I wish I had" is something I will be forever proud.

Yes, the price of success is high but the pain of regret is so much higher.

I soon became committed to leading from the center, while forming a strong identity in the process of creating my brand. Serving others and staying true to the integrity of who I was and wanted to become was very important to me.

Because of this mentality I was able to instill this mindset in my son. He will carry on my legacy knowing that he too can be, do and have whatever his heart desires.

Notes

CHAPTER 6

Giving Yourself Permission

I knew the importance of guarding my heart but more importantly, understanding the results of being 100 percent committed to my dreams. I started my Mary Kay business at the age of 21 and was single, so I had already made the decision to be successful long before I got married.

I also made the decision to be self-sufficient and independently wealthy on my own, not counting on someone else to take care of me. I feel this was a curse and a blessing. It was a curse because I allowed someone to become dependent on me, but also a blessing because it kept me going and pressing forward in the midst of major storms and adversity. The detriment in all of this was that I kept putting a blanket over the fact that I was miserable in my marriage, starving for the love, affection and support every woman wants from her spouse.

I thought that if I gave more, did more and poured more into it, which he would reciprocate but that didn't happen. My cup became drained very quickly. The one thing that did fill my cup was my Mary Kay business. My clients, consultants and sister Directors were my number one support system.

However, as I grew, my marriage was falling apart and becoming more toxic and unhealthy. It can be very difficult if one spouse is growing and the other chooses to stand still and settle. I see this in so many relationships. Where the spouse

When the pain of remaining the same becomes greater than the pain of change, you will step over the line, and become bold enough to make the necessary changes.

Shannon M. Tobin

will blame the Mary Kay opportunity for their marriage falling apart instead of facing the mirror and seeing that it takes work from both parties and a commitment to grow, accept and respect one another.

One thing I know to be true: you can't help someone who doesn't want to help themselves. I couldn't, nor did I want to try to fix someone anymore. I was emotionally, spiritually, mentally and physically drained. God sent me many life preservers and rescue boats, but until I saw that they were for me, nothing changed.

My decision to get off the fence and end my marriage was solidified while vacationing in California. Three painful incidents occurred, and I decided I couldn't do it anymore. The moment I dropped my husband and son off at the airport, I knew I was done!

In my mind, my marriage was over, and I would be going home to begin the divorce proceedings. Never in my 13-year relationship had I ever considered being unfaithful, nor would I ever be tempted to have an affair. However, something else happened that shouldn't have. Maybe it was because I was sucked dry. My heart felt like it had been put through the blender, and spit out! I had no more love to give, nor did I understand the difference between love and lust.

It's amazing how some people can see that from a mile away and they choose to take advantage of the situation? Well, my former coach was on his way to our leadership conference to speak at several Mary Kay National Area events, so we had arranged a time to meet for dinner. That dinner turned into an overnight get together. I think you get the picture. And, sadly, for some reason,

I didn't feel any guilt or shame. However, I knew the next steps were going to be the most difficult. I prayed the entire flight home asking God to open the door, and he did. That was just another confirmation that his hands were on this the entire time. My husband knew when I dropped him and my son off at the airport that we were done. He knew I was rocked by the two major verbal blow-ups he started in public, plus slapping me with an urgent notice that I had to pay his personal visa bill that was past due. Because he didn't have money to pay for it, I had no choice, so he said. And to top it off, all three of these incidents happened with my son present.

I was so angry I could have spit nails, but because my son was present, I had to hold back and bite my tongue.

I arrived home around 11:00 p.m. from travelling all day. I was exhausted and missed my son, so I decided to go and lie in his bed and cuddle. I also didn't want to see or be in the presence of his father, as I was still very angry and bitter. He woke me up around 2:00 a.m. and asked me to come to the living room to talk and that he had to ask me something. There was no apology. He just said, "Do you love me?" I looked at him straight in the eye and said "No! I want you to leave! I'm done!" Of course, the rage began; things were thrown and broken. This wasn't the first time. I even had to go as far as picking up the phone and threatening to call 911 because I feared what he was going to do. My son slept through the entire thing. He had become so accustomed to his father's yelling and cursing that it didn't even wake him up. This was the beginning of very turbulent and rocky times.

So, of course, the first thing he did was to try and blame me by accusing me of having an affair, although he still hadn't come to grips with telling me that he had been unfaithful to me, when I was nine months pregnant. For five years, he had denied it. I knew what happened but he would never admit it. The downward spiral started before Cole was born. Sadly, I didn't have the courage or stamina to talk to my family about it and kept silent and continued to cover up the truth, lies and pain of what I was living. It wasn't until after we separated that he admitted being unfaithful.

When I look back, I can clearly see what an empty shell I had become, and that I was sucked dry of any love and loyalty. I felt the way he treated me on our vacation was despicable, and I didn't care anymore about us or what people would think. I had no clue where this path would lead me, but I did know that God would be there as my rock. You sure find out who your supporters are when you go through a tragedy or crisis. There wasn't one friend who asked "Why are you doing this?" They couldn't understand what took me so long! I'll focus on the positive blessings and new friendships that were formed. It wouldn't be fair to try and name all of the people who supported me through this terrible time, so I won't attempt to, in fear I'd miss someone. I will say however, Thank you from the bottom of a very grateful heart!

I've learned so much from author and public speaker Larry Diangi! His book: Overcoming rejection will make you rich, taught me the importance of building momentum in your business and getting your plane up in the air so when the time comes that you need to use your autopilot and coast, you can. I'm so grateful that I worked hard when I could! As a result of hard work and dedication for many years, I was able to take the time necessary to heal, process, and be there for Cole. I also got him into therapy right away. The best gift I gave myself was the gift of time while leaning on my faith. It gave me the strength to model discipline, instill values and speak life into my son when it wasn't visible.

According to Saint Augustine, "Faith is to believe what you do not see. The reward of faith is to see what you've believed."

The ability to bounce-back and not allow circumstances control my desired outcome had to become my mentality! This meant having an unwavering belief system and 100 percent commitment no matter what.

This is another reason why I'm so passionate about showing women that they too can weather any storm that comes their way and thrive. It's so easy to point a finger and blame others. It's time we take 100 percent responsibility for where we are today. So often we blame events, people or circumstances in our life but we must rise above all of this and say: "I choose to be a victor of my circumstances, not a victim!"

We all got our stuff! We are either in a crisis, on our way out of a crisis or going into a crisis. If we all put our challenges in the middle of the table, we would want our own back, wouldn't you agree?

If you want major changes to take place in your life, then you must make some major changes now.

The definition of insanity is doing the same things over and over again and expecting different results!

When the pain of remaining the same becomes greater than the pain of change, you'll step over the line, become bold in your faith, and make the changes necessary.

It all starts with a commitment first by choosing to step over the line. This means having the attitude that quitting is not an option, no matter how tough it gets.

When I think of commitment, I think of Mary Kay Ash. One month before she opened the doors to her company, her husband died of a heart attack. Her attorney told her to liquidate everything and turn it into cash. Did she listen? No. She was committed!

It takes 100 percent commitment to move mountains and achieve your dreams. It's the motivator that moves you forward no matter what. It's making the decision before it happens. Committed individuals don't fall apart when there are bumps in the road.

Do they have fears? You bet! As long as you're pursuing your dreams, you will always have fears and failures. Fears cause you to procrastinate, if you're not committed. You have to commit to take action and not live in your fear. You can either feed your fear or feed your faith.

I'm more afraid of the fear of regret; aren't you? Accept the fact that as long as you're going to stretch you will have fears.

Replace that fear with your power of faith!

O.K., now it's time to talk about failure. Let's call them "successful failures." Mary Kay used to always say, "We fail forward to success!"

> Exchange your rear view mirror for a set of binoculars. God is looking at your future and has a great destiny for your life.
>
> Shannon M. Tobin

Be willing to look at what failure teaches us—
there are lessons to learn. Be willing to fall down
nine times and get up 10 times. My mantra is:

"I'M NEVER DOWN,
I'M EITHER UP OR GETTING BACK UP!"

Train yourself to think of failures as mile mark-
ers getting you closer to your goals.

They strengthen you and redirect you.
Appreciate them and allow them to teach you
and move forward.

Okay so now that we've addressed the whole
fear and failure stuff, write this down:

I'VE GOT TO FIND MY PURPOSE.

Once you find the purpose and can articulate
it, you will become passionately inspired deep
within. As Gandhi advises: You've got to be the
change you want to see!

The goal is never to change who you are but
to change what you do, so you can be who you
really are.

You need to take your dreams out of the closet
and put them into action.

What is the number one thing that holds people back? What keeps us in a place of fear from
living out our purpose?

I believe it is permission or a lack there of.

We don't give ourselves permission to be who
we already are. It sounds simple, but it's true! If
you've been fearful of taking the next step, of going to the next level, of letting go of things you

need to let go of, you probably haven't given yourself permission to be who you already are.

Give yourself permission to be at peace by putting yourself out front.

Give yourself permission to be excellent; permission to be unique; permission to be smart and beautiful; permission to have an impact on the lives of others; permission to change the world with the unique gifts and talents God has given to you. The unique thing about the word permission is that it implies you have unfiltered access to a special place that has been designed for you. You have to have a key to access that special place. God gave the key to you as gifts.

That place is available for you, but you have to give yourself access and not self-sabotage. To live a life of permission to be at peace, to have amazing friendships and relationships, so you can serve people. You must give yourself permission to dream bigger! God wants you to live out your dreams.

It's not someone else who's blocking you or holding you back. There might be things you have to let go of, but you first have to give yourself permission to believe that you deserve more.

When you determine that "the best" is the only place that you can arrive at, everything else that is less than the best will be eliminated. You must know that the best is inside you.

You're going to have to choose what you will eliminate. Everything and everybody cannot go with you into your next season. Not if you've truly given yourself permission to live life.

You were designed uniquely. Your dreams have not been forgotten. You are exactly where you are supposed to be. Everything that you have been

Quit looking to others to affirm you and the path you're on. If you've put God behind the wheel, nothing else matters.

Shannon M. Tobin

through and the challenges and obstacles that you've encountered all happened for a specific reason. You can look at your circumstances as a victim or a victor knowing that God needed you to go through this in order for you to be able to help someone else who will experience the same challenges.

It's time to stop blaming and playing the victim. Only you have the key to unlock the door to this secret place.

I pray you will have the boldness that will be required to use that key. You will have the right mindset by pouring positive things into your life. God has pre-destined plans for you. It's time for you to give yourself permission.

The best is in store for you, so give yourself permission to be brilliant, excellent and live the life God has planned for you.

Notes

CHAPTER 7

Thriving In A Surviving World

It seems to be a constant battle between thriving and surviving. How do we change gears and turn our attention and focus towards thriving and away from merely surviving? How do we embrace an abundant mentality and live life the best way possible in spite of our circumstances?

There are three common traits in successful people:

#1   They are willing to work

#2   They are willing to risk

#3   They are willing to sacrifice

Are you truly ready to stand in your personal power and turn your business and life around, because a dream without work is nothing more than a fantasy?

Yes, effort = results, but first you may need to have a mindset shift. You can have all the skill in the world, but if there's something holding you back, you need to find out what it is; then get it fixed. It could happen overnight, or it may take a little longer. The process will be much quicker when you get the assistance of professional help. Don't do it alone.

It's imperative to develop an 'It's none of my business what you think of me' attitude and know your purpose! This is the substance of why you want what you want.

Do not conform any longer to the pattern of this world, but be transformed by the renewing of your mind.

Romans 12:2

Yes, it's highly possible that you'll need to sacrifice some things for a short period of time, such as: not watching television every night, or sacrifice a few hours a week with your kids, knowing that they will get to go to Disney on a dream vacation as the pay off (for example). I'd rather pay now and play later, than play now and pay later, wouldn't you?

Winners don't mind the price they have to pay in order to achieve success. Many fail because they're not willing to pay the price of victory. Think about this for a minute. What are you teaching your children by thinking and dreaming small? What message are you sending by not taking chances and being willing to work risk and sacrifice for what you want?

10 Things Winners Do Differently

This can be the difference maker on how to thrive in life versus merely surviving.

Anyone can give up, and lots of people do, because it's the easiest thing in the world to do. But to keep going when everyone would understand if you stopped - that's what winners do differently. In fact, this is the most significant principle of winning. Because without this kind of determination and persistence, the first nine points I'm going to share wouldn't matter. But when you combine determination and persistence, as described in point number 10 below, with each of the other nine points that's when the real magic happens.

On their relentless road to victory, winners...

1. Take 100 percent responsibility – Your life is your statement to the world, representing your values, beliefs and dreams. It is yours

to create, to enjoy or not, to fight or to be at peace. In the end, the very best years of your life will be the ones in which you decide your problems are your own. You do not blame them on your parents, society or the economy. You realize that you control your own destiny.

2. Focus on the controllable – Life is a balance between what we can and cannot control. Life does not owe you anything; it has already given you everything you need. Freedom is not overcoming what you think stands in your way; it is understanding that what is in your way is part of the way.

3. Eliminate the wrong things – The true price of anything you do is the amount of time you exchange for it. If something you're doing or thinking isn't fixing or improving the situation, then it's wasting your time. There comes a point when you have to choose between turning the page and closing the book, so you can begin to write a new one.

4. Maintain control – Start shaping your own days. Start walking your own walk. This journey is yours. You know you were born, and you know you will die. The 'in between' is all up to you. Stop wishing and start doing. Either you run your days, or your days will run you.

5. Keep good company – It's not always where you are in life, but who you have by your side that matters most. Some people drain you and others provide soul food. Be sure to get in the company of those who feed your spirit

and give the gift of your absence to those who do not appreciate your presence.

6. Think constructively – Change your thoughts and you change your reality. Our thoughts are the makers of our moods, the inventors of our dreams, and the creators of our will. That is why you must sort through them carefully and choose to respond only to those that will help you build the life you want, and the outlook you want to hold as you're living it.

7. Conquer oneself – Being yourself is the foundation of happiness. Knowing yourself is the foundation of wisdom. Pushing yourself is the foundation of success. It is better to conquer yourself is these ways, than to win a hundred battles elsewhere in life.

8. Practice self-love – We need to fix ourselves before we fix others. Caring for you is not an act of self-indulgence; it's an act of self-respect. The day will finally come when you have to accept that you need to be your own caretaker. There will be times when you'll have to work hard to mother yourself with the compassion and patience that any messed up kid would need. Doing so will prove to be a great challenge, but a happier life is your reward.

9. Work through the pain – One day this pain will make sense to you. Sometimes it takes the worst pain to bring about the best change. The strongest people you know became strong because of the pain they once faced, and conquered. So in spite of all the put-downs and negativity you've heard from others in your

life, stay focused on your goals, and remember that how you rise up is no one else's business but your own.

10. Keep going – No matter what you do, no matter how many times you screw up and think to yourself that there's no point to carry on, and no matter how many people tell you that you can't do it – keep going. Pick yourself back up. Don't quit. Don't quit, because a few months from now you will be so much closer to your goal than you are now. Focus on the road ahead. Do something today for which your future self will thank you.

Notes

CHAPTER 8

The Guy Factor

I t very common for women who have left toxic, controlling, and/or abusive relationships to enter into one just the same as the one they just left. Why would that be? Because she didn't properly heal the first set of wounds, nor did she seek proper counseling to ensure it wouldn't happen again.

Unfortunately, the first coach I hired, to assist me in the process of discovering my identity, was no different. I had 'sucker' written all over my face! Or maybe should I say 'Miss Vulnerable.' He was the devil disguised in a different suit.

He got to know me better than anyone. He knew my weaknesses, strengths and earned my trust, therefore my heart. And that gave him the ammunition to be able to take from me what he wanted.

It wasn't until I was willing to face him dead-on and question the integrity of his work that I realized his true character, just by his reaction to my accusations. A person's true character will always show up during times of question, whether they respond or react and defend, with their ammunition ready to fire.

This was a lesson that not only cost me thousands of dollars but also caused me to have an even less trust in men.

The only person I was hurting was myself, so I realized quickly that in order for me to be able to move on and create joy in my life, I needed to let go and forgive. Forgive myself most importantly

Be strong when you are weak, brave when you are scared, and humble when you are victorious.

Author unknown

and then forgive the two men who had hurt me so deeply. One day, I realized that their actions had nothing to do with me, but everything to do with them. I began to pray for abundant blessings on their lives and found the compassionate side of me again, which was lost or should I say stripped from me.

The devil works in mysterious ways, but God is powerful and mighty and will win every time if we 100 percent give it to Him!

To be able to help other women develop confidence, self-worth and financial independence that is needed to stand up and step out in faith has now become a strong purpose in my life.

We all have baggage; however, I'm a firm believer that you need one to two years to heal after leaving a toxic marriage/relationship before entering a new one. You can't discover who you truly are while being influenced by someone else. Nor will you face the mirror the same way.

Don't rush into anything. There's great joy and peace in learning to love you. Learn to love yourself for who you are instead of trying to be someone you're not in order to please another.

I know I have a purpose greater than myself. I'm not raising my son to survive in the world. I'm raising him to become a vital part in changing the world.

In the process of learning and understanding that I was in survival mode for so long, I realized how important it is for me to embrace thriving in all areas of my life, including being alone and learning to love myself for who I am. I knew that in order for me to attract the right energy and people into my life, I had to go through this process alone and without any distractions. Did I

You have the opportunity to turn every wound into a weapon and every mess into a message, if you allow time and God to heal you.

Shannon M. Tobin

think it would take two and half years and a lot of mirror facing? I had no clue. The journey of discovering who I am went from being a painful experience to a liberating and beautiful one. It is something I will cherish forever.

The biggest mistake both women and men make is entering a new relationship before they've healed, recovered and learned the lessons from the last one. Most people don't want to be alone, nor do they want to face the mirror and dig deep. This is why there are so many dysfunctional relationships.

Once I became aware of this, I took responsibility for making sure this didn't happen again. I took the necessary steps to become whole, strong and powerful internally, so the next relationship I entered would start off on the right path. This was the first time in my life that I really embraced this process. Not only do I feel I have a new lease on life, but I'm clear about what I will and what I won't accept from a partner.

When I became solid and true to myself, I began to look at things, people and relationships in a totally different light. I also saw the importance of building a solid foundation and forming a friendship first. "First come friendship, then comes love"

Notes

CHAPTER 9

Love 'You' More

When I began to love myself was the day I went from survival mode to thriving!

My dear girlfriend, Nathalie Delisle, who I believe came into my life by divine appointment, shared this with me as I was preparing to speak at a seminar in Toronto in July 2012. I'm so grateful for her friendship, support and unconditional love during the most difficult storm in my life.

Charlie Chaplain wrote this poem on his 70th birthday:

AS I BEGAN TO LOVE MYSELF
by Charlie Chaplin

As I began to love myself I found that anguish and emotional suffering are only warning signs that I was living against my own truth. Today, I know, this is AUTHENTICITY.

As I began to love myself I understood how much it can offend somebody, as I try to force my desires on this person, even though I knew the time was not right and the person was not ready for it, and even though this person was me. Today I call it RESPECT.

As I began to love myself I stopped craving for a different life, and I could see that everything that surrounded me was inviting me to grow. Today I call it MATURITY.

As I began to love myself I understood that at any circumstance, I am in the right place

> You owe the world your gifts; you just have to find out how to use them.
>
> Shannon M. Tobin

Don't ever forget

your greatness!

YOU matter, and

YOU count!

Shannon M. Tobin

at the right time, and everything happens at the exactly right moment, so I could be calm. Today I call it SELF-CONFIDENCE.

As I began to love myself I quit steeling my own time, and I stopped designing huge projects for the future. Today, I only do what brings me joy and happiness, things I love to do and that make my heart cheer, and I do them in my own way and in my own rhythm. Today I call it SIMPLICITY.

As I began to love myself I freed myself of anything that is no good for my health – food, people, things, situations, and everything that drew me down and away from myself. At first I called this attitude a healthy egoism. Today I know it is LOVE OF ONESELF.

As I began to love myself I quit trying to always be right, and ever since I was wrong less of the time. Today I discovered that is MODESTY.

As I began to love myself I refused to go on living in the past and worry about the future. Now, I only live for the moment, where EVERYTHING is happening. Today I live each day, day by day, and I call it FULFILLMENT.

As I began to love myself I recognized that my mind can disturb me and it can make me sick. But as I connected it to my heart, my mind became a valuable ally. Today I call this connection WISDOM OF THE HEART.

We no longer need to fear arguments, confrontations or any kind of problems with ourselves or others. Even stars collide, and out of their crashing new worlds are born.

Today I know THAT IS LIFE!"

This poem has had such powerful meaning in my life. The most difficult task for me in all of this was forgiving myself: forgiving myself for not leaving earlier; forgiving myself for allowing someone to continually belittle and put me down; forgiving myself for ignoring the red flags that brought more heartache and pain into my life.

There were days during my marriage when all I could do was to block my current situation out. I just put up and shut up until I began to see the side effects this was having on my son. When he, at the age of five, didn't even flinch in the midst of his father's rage. That was when I knew something needed to change. I always said that I wanted to leave a legacy for my son but surely not one like this.

The definition of insanity is doing the same things over and over again and expecting different results. I talk a lot about this when I train Mary Kay consultants, but I wasn't following it in my personal life. This was a wakeup call for me.

When the pain of remaining the same became greater than the pain of change, I stepped across the line and became bold enough to make the changes necessary.

It all began with a commitment to myself and started with stepping across the line. Settling for less than what God had in store for me was not going to be the way of my life anymore.

It takes 100 percent commitment to move mountains and achieve your dreams! This commitment to self is the motivator that moves you forward no matter what. It's making a concrete decision before random events happen.

Committed individuals don't fall apart when there are bumps in the road. Do they have fears?

You bet. As long as you're pursuing your dreams, you will always have fears and failures. Fears cause you to procrastinate if you're not committed. You have to commit to take action and not live in fear. You can either feed your fear or feed your faith.

As I became more afraid of the regret, I replaced that fear with the power of faith!

Don't wish it was easier; wish you were better.

Jim Rohn

Notes

CHAPTER 10

Independent But Ready

I used to think that portraying a perfect image for others was so important until I realized that when I was at the top of my game, number one in the country, I was unhappy, unfulfilled and an empty person.

When I look at my life now, I can see and feel what it's truly like to live a life of freedom: freedom to be; freedom to do; freedom to have; freedom to live; freedom to give and freedom to give. This has become my obsession. It wasn't about portraying that perfect image anymore or living someone else's agenda, but being true to who I am and living my purpose.

When I became transparent and open to sharing the story of how I overcame adversity, challenges and internal battles, I began to inspire others to break free from surviving and move into to thriving in all areas of their lives as well.

I believe there are no mistakes, so whether you purchased this book, or were given this as a gift, I hope it has enriched your life and has given you the courage to make necessary changes to break free from the chains are holding you back from truly living your life's purpose.

Until you can look at yourself in the mirror and love what you see, you won't be able to truly allow someone else to love you or fully give your love to someone else.

This is a journey that takes time, commitment and guidance from the right people. Another reason why so many men and women exit one toxic

> Success in life is ultimately determined by our response to hardship and failure.
>
> Stepp Stevens Sydnor

relationship and immediately enter another is because they haven't taken the time to truly heal, forgive and love themselves. It took me two and a half years. I'm now able to allow the right person into my life and won't bring the garbage from my past into a new relationship. This is a mistake so many people make and is often the reason why their second relationship fails.

Just as 'success is an inside job,' so is, loving yourself.

Notes

CHAPTER 11

Family Matters

Children Learn What They Live

If a child lives with criticism -
 he learns to condemn
If a child lives with hostility -
 he learns to fight
If a child lives with ridicule -
 he learns to be shy
If a child lives with shame -
 he learns to feel guilty
If a child lives with tolerance -
 he learns to be patient
If a child lives with encouragement -
 he learns confidence
If a child lives with praise -
 he learns to appreciate
If a child lives with fairness -
 he learns justice
If a child lives with security -
 he learns to have faith
If a child lives with approval -
 he learns to like himself
If a child lives with acceptance and friendship -
 he learns to find love in the world.

Dorothy Law Nolte
Copyright © 1972/1975 by Dorothy Law Nolte

Speak life into your home and into the people around you today. Your words are more meaningful to them than anyone else's words.

Shannon M. Tobin

The hardest job in the world is the best job in the world: being a mom! Cole is my purpose, my 'why' and the reason I keep going during the most difficult times.

How could I ever encourage him to stay the course, if I allow the actions and opinions of others to control my mental state? The best gift I've given to my son is to show him by example that no matter what happens, he needs to hold his faith tight, keep going and never give up on his dreams. I want him to know that success in life comes with a price, but, if you do it right, the price is insignificant. The best gift we can give our kids is the gift of choice. When we teach them to live free and true to themselves, we are teaching them values and giving them the confidence to know they'll never walk alone.

It's taken me 41 years to break the mold of conformity and to be true to myself. The reward has been worth every ounce of pain, including all the blood, sweat and tears that come with it. I will do everything in my power to help Cole see his God-given talents and abilities early on in life. I will encourage and support him in the process as he discovers his own flight pattern. A legacy he will be able to pass on to his own children.

Note from the Author:

There are no mistakes. I hope and pray this book is valuable to you and that my story will inspire you, giving you courage to take on the transformation process necessary to discover your own flight pattern, and that you'll pay it forward.

For this reason, I have chosen to donate the profits from my book to support funding for my nonprofit foundation: Dare to be you. It will create scholarships for teen girls and boys to attend weekend workshops on how to discover their own flight patterns.

We can choose to be part of the problem or part of the solution. I hope you'll join me in this movement to empower our next generation, so they can thrive in a surviving world.

Special Thanks:

This book would never have been written if it weren't for the encouragement, guidance and belief from my life coach Tony Gaskins Jr. I've become even more passionate and committed to leaving a mark of significance on the world by fulfilling God's vision for my life because of him. He's elevated my thinking and vision to a whole new level, which has brought about my next chapter in the story of my life. This includes starting of a nonprofit foundation which will support and fund so many great causes.

To my mom, the greatest role model and strongest woman I know: thank you for the example you provide for Sean and I, as well as so many other single moms. It was never about you but always for a greater purpose.

To my brother Sean and sister-in-law Asami: I value both of you, and admire you for the wonderful couple and parents you are to Ayame and Kevin.

To my National Sales Director Emeritus, Heather Armstrong: You've poured your unconditional love into my life for 29 years and allowed me to run my own race, sometimes solo. You've given me the roadmap to living a life of significance, and now I am committed to carrying on your legacy - a gift I will cherish forever.

To my Million Dollar National girlfriend Bernice Boe Malin: You have mentored and paved the way for me and countless others. I feel truly blessed to have learned from you all these years and to be able to call you my friend.

To my Mary Kay sisters and girlfriends outside of Mary Kay: I cherish and appreciate each and every one of you. Many of you stood beside me every step of the way and encouraged me to spread my wings and fly, never judging me in the process of discovering my life's purpose. Thank you!

To all the naysayers and people who wanted to see me fail, crumble and break. You gave me the strength, drive and perseverance to take the road less travelled and stay the course.

To the Independent National Sales Director who said she didn't have the time to take a picture with me: You taught me a valuable lesson - that everyone wears a sign around their neck that says "Make me feel important" and that our words either elevate or destroy a person's inner spirit.

The final chapters of my book were inspired and written while vacationing in New Denver, British Columbia at my dear friends Wally and Mary Fulko's home. Being surrounded by the mountains in awe of God's work inspired me beyond measure! I cherish you both and feel blessed to have known you my entire life.

Thank you Debra Hicks, my dear friend for many years, for capturing the awe inspiring photo of me on the top of Wilson Creek falls. I will always be grateful for the push you gave me to step out of my comfort zone.

And last but not least, to Michelle Snively-Jefferies. You painted my "transformation" so beautifully and I'm blessed to be able to share your gifts and talents with the world by having your art work as part of my book cover.

The Ultimate reward of Forgiveness is love of self.
It is a love that will provide you with the courage to move confidently toward a better future.
It starts with releasing any burdens from the past
so you can reveal a worthy and deserving human
being capable of manifesting your true greatness.

After a while you learn the difference,
Between holding a hand and chaining a soul,
And you learn that love doesn't mean leaning
And company doesn't always mean security,
And you begin to learn that kisses aren't contracts
    and presents aren't promises,
And you begin to accept your defeats
With your head up and your eyes ahead,
With the grace of an adult, not the grief of a child,
And you learn to build all your roads on today
Because tomorrow's ground is too uncertain for
    plans, and futures have a way of falling down
    in midflight.
After a while you learn that even sunshine burns
if you get too much.
So plant your own garden and decorate your own
    soul, Instead of waiting for someone to bring
    you flowers and you learn that you really can
    endure...
That you really are strong. And you really do have
    worth.

Veronica A. Shoffstall
©1971 Veronica A. Shoffstall

You put yourself
in prison when
you don't
forgive.

Joyce Meyer

It serves no one for you to hold back and not bring to the world all that you have to offer.

Epilogues

By Ari Randall

"A person is never quite so near success as when that which he calls 'failure' has overtaken him, for it is on occasions of this sort that one is forced to think. If one thinks accurately, and with persistence, he discovers that so-called failure usually is nothing more than a signal to re-arm himself with a new plan or purpose. Most real failures are due to limitations which men set up in their minds. If they had the courage to go one step further, they would discover their error."
Napoleon Hill

I read this phrase for the first time today, at the perfect time in my life. For the last three to four months, I've been working daily to live extraordinarily. I have had small successes, for which I am very grateful. But I have also had a few falls. I can stand firm on this day and say that I am even MORE thankful and grateful for these small failures because they have given me a clear picture of what I don't want and helped me focus on the things I do want, as well showing me what I should be doing to attain success.

The only way to make this clear to yourself is to accept a mirror in front of your face in the form of self awareness and feedback from someone you value.

I have the most wonderful coach and mentor in Shannon Tobin, who helps by putting the mirror in front of me. This mirror is not meant to be a bad thing at all; it's meant as a tool to help me grow. And that it has. Just like when you are making a batch of cookies and have to add baking powder as well as chocolate chips - some ingredients doesn't taste very good alone. However, when you combine them in the right mix, the result is so worth it.

I can't stress enough how vital Shannon's daily mentoring has been for me. It comes down to one simple truth: If you want to succeed at something you are passionate about, listen to someone who has been where you are and is now where you want to be!

Thank you, Shannon, for letting me fall on my own, so that I can always be empowered to get up again on my own. My journey continues . . .

By Scarlett Walker-Simpson

Shannon is a light shining in the dark, and God is using her in a mighty and powerful way to empower, inspire and lead others to overcome obstacles and become their best. Her own journey has brought her from darkness to a shining life that is impacting others in an amazing way. Her wisdom and insight is God- inspired and she is changing lives!

Scarlett Walker-Simpson is a Senior National Sales Director for Mary Kay Cosmetics U.S

Don't rush the climb!
The journey to the top is always the most beautiful

Photo taken by Debra Hicks

Learn more about discovering your own flight pattern
www.shannonmtobin.com